What Made Them So Brave?

M. Basilea Schlink

Evangelical Sisterhood of Mary

Phoenix, Arizona, U.S.A.

Copies of WHAT MADE THEM SO BRAVE? are available from:

Evangelical Sisterhood of Mary
9849 North 40th Street
Phoenix, AZ 85028
U.S.A.

Evangelical Sisterhood of Mary
Tracy, New Brunswick E0G 3C0
Canada

Evangelical Sisterhood of Mary
447 A Pennant Hills Road
Pennant Hills, N.S.W. 2120
Australia

Evangelical Sisterhood of Mary
90 Valleyview Crescent
Edmonton, Alberta T5R 5T1
Canada

Evangelical Sisterhood of Mary
17 Gills Hill Lane
Radlett, Herts, WD7 8DE
England

ISBN 3 87209 655 9

Original Title: *Jesu Kleine Getreue*
First German Edition — 1977
First English Edition — 1978
Fourth English Printing — 1980

Printed in the United States of America.

Table of Contents

Dear Children,

You have a very special place in my heart and I often pray for you, since you are having such a hard time nowadays. Many of you are sad and afraid, laughed at and ridiculed and no longer know what to do — yes, some of you may even have thought that you would rather not go on living. But believe me, you are especially dear to the Lord Jesus! It makes Him very sad to think of you living in such dark times. But this time of darkness won't last long. And afterwards the light will shine all the brighter, for then our Lord Jesus will reveal who He is — the King of kings!

However, in the midst of these hard times that you have to live through, the Lord Jesus wants to fill your hearts with comfort. I shall be telling you about this in the book and shall continue to pray for you, so that you may be brave soldiers for Jesus, soldiers of love.

With very best wishes,

Mother Basilea

You know that although our Lord Jesus loves us very much, He is attacked and hated practically all over the world today. For this reason He is counting on you children as never before to witness to Him, to stand up for Him and prove Him your love, as Angela did.

Angela is ten years old. She lives in an Eastern European country where the Christian faith is oppressed. Her teacher wanted to stamp out the faith in every child who still believed in God. She was especially unkind to Angela, for she knew that the girl often went to church.

Then just before Christmas the teacher thought up a trap. She said to Angela, "When your parents call you, what do you do?"

"I obey and come," replied Angela timidly.

"And what happens when your parents call the chimney sweep?"

"He comes," said Angela.

"Good, my child. The chimney sweep comes, because he is real. But let us say that your parents call your grandfather, who is no longer alive. Will he come?"

"No, I don't think so."

"And when we call Rumpelstiltskin or Little Red Riding Hood, what happens then?"

"Nobody will come. They're only in fairy tales."

"Very good," said the teacher triumphantly. "You see, children, people who are alive come when you call them, but not people who don't exist or are no longer alive. Is that clear?"

"Yes," the class replied in unison.

"Now suppose you call the Baby Jesus. Do you believe, Angela, that the Baby Jesus will hear you when you call it?"

Angela replied with the utmost conviction, "Yes, I believe He will hear me."

"We shall see!" retorted the teacher. "If the Baby Jesus really does exist, it will hear you call. So all of you call together, 'Come, Baby Jesus, come!'"

Alarm and terror gripped the children. As a matter of fact, a number of them believed in God. What were they to do now? Then something totally unexpected happened. With a leap Angela stood in the middle of her classmates and cried out with shining eyes, "Yes, let's all call together and ask Him to come." The children rose from their seats and in their distress called out, desperate and yet filled with hope, "Come, Baby Jesus! Come, Baby Jesus!"

And what happened? Before the teacher could begin to scoff, the Baby Jesus really did appear – in a bright ray of light. Not only the children but also the teacher saw Him. For the children it was a wonderful answer to prayer and they were overjoyed, but for the teacher it was a terrible shock. She turned as white as a sheet and screamed, "It came!" Then she dashed out, slamming the door behind her. But even though she experienced this miracle of God, she did not turn from her wicked ways. In the end she was taken to a psychiatric hospital, because she kept on repeating, "It came! It came!"[1] By contrast, Angela and the other children who believed in God learnt from this incident that when you take Jesus' side, He will take yours. And since this was an emergency situation, Jesus acted in a special way.

Perhaps you are thinking, "I too would like to have the courage to stand up for Jesus when others laugh at Him, make fun of Him or say He is dead. But how can I get this courage?" Later on I shall tell you.

[1] see notes at back of book

Talking to Jesus Day by Day

Now why do you think Angela knew for sure that the teacher was wrong when she scoffed and said Jesus was dead and wouldn't come when He was called? Where did she find the courage to call out confidently in front of this teacher, "Come, Baby Jesus, come!"? Angela was able to do this, because she used to pray to Jesus every day. She would talk with the Good Shepherd as His beloved little lamb. This wasn't the first time that she had called to Him when she was in distress. She had always prayed to Him. And every time she prayed, she knew that He was present and very close. This is how she found the courage to call upon Jesus in front of the scoffing teacher.

Angela firmly believed that Jesus would hear her prayer. She was convinced, because she knew that Jesus has a special love for children. When you pray, you can really sense this deep down in your heart. Indeed, He even said once, "Let the children come to Me." He took them in His arms and blessed them and to this very day He does the same. Not only the little ones, but every single one of you can know for sure that you can come to Him. His arms are wide open. He loves you. Yes, He really loves each one of you. And since you have to live in a dark world today, where fear and terror abound, Jesus and the heavenly Father love you all the more. So come and talk to Jesus in prayer.

Whoever knows that he is dearly loved takes care not to hurt the one who loves him so much. No doubt, Angela always brought Jesus her sins and any naughty thing she did, so that He would not be sad about her. She would let all her sinful stains be washed away by His blood, which was shed for her. For as the Bible says, His blood cleanses us from all sin. And so Angela experienced that she was completely cleansed. In a way it's like washing dirty clothes – afterwards they are so clean that not a spot can be seen on them.

And so each time Angela would come away from prayer with a light heart and skipping for joy. She had discovered how happy Jesus can make us. Being naughty only makes us unhappy and others too – our parents, brothers and sisters, our teachers and everyone else around us.

When Jesus' loyal young followers ever anew talk with their Lord, who not only forgives them their sins, but also helps them to change, their love for Him will grow with each new prayer. And as their love grows, so will their courage, and they will be able to follow the Lord Jesus, be loyal to Him in every situation and resist the devil when he tempts them.

He came to earth to find you,
From sin to set you free.
For us in love He suffered
And died on Calvary.

His hand He's stretching out.
Won't you trust Him today?
His pow'r can drive your troubles,
Distress and fears away.

NJ No.10

Mike Doesn't Go Along

Last summer Mike asked the Lord Jesus to come into his heart. He is now eight years old. His classmates were planning a mischievous prank and they tried to make Mike come with them.

"Don't be a spoilsport," they said, "or else you'll have to pay for it."

But Mike refused. At the given time he didn't turn up. Instead he helped his mother and went shopping for her at the grocers. The next day his classmates were very angry with him. They made fun of him and even hit him – all because he didn't go along. Mike felt very dejected, for every new day at school brought him more suffering.

One day as they were all eating lunch in the big dining hall – children and teachers together, as is customary in Mike's country – the principal's voice suddenly came over the loudspeaker. The lady who worked at the local grocers rang up to give a good report about Mike, since he was always so friendly and polite when he went shopping. After lunch Mike's classmates who had taunted and hit him came up to him and asked what he had done to earn so much praise. They then said, "Mike, we wanted to keep on hitting you, to let you know what a spoilsport you are. But we can't, because Jesus always helps you."

What an encouragement this was for Mike to continue following Jesus! And whenever something was said or done against Jesus, he wanted to take a stand for Him.

Shortly after this incident a magician came to the school. For just a small entrance fee you could see the magician performing his clever tricks and weird magic. But Mike said, "I won't go inside. Magic is a bad thing and it makes Jesus sad. And because I love Jesus, I don't want to see it."

Jesus won't forsake me,
He's with me always;
I will love and trust Him,
He leads not astray.
Jesus, O Love Everlasting.

Mike grew stronger and stronger, for he wanted to live to please the Lord Jesus and not his classmates. He wanted to be one of Jesus' loyal young followers. Do you want to be one too?

Jesus,
I would
stand
beside You,
Though
so many
now
forsake You.
May
I follow
faithfully,
Though
but weak
and
small
I be.

The Red Flag and a Piece of Golden Chalk

To His children, His loyal followers, who are prepared to suffer for Him, Jesus gave a promise a long time ago. He said that they were not to worry about what to say when they were called to stand up for Him. When that time comes, they will be given the words to say (Matthew 10:19). This was the experience of two girls who lived in Eastern Europe.

Six-year-old Maria was in her first year at school. Because she continued to pray and tell the other children about Jesus, she was made to stay after school one day. All the teachers came together. Once and for all Maria was to be "re-educated". The teachers were going to question her and she would have to answer them. Maria was given a piece of chalk and told, "If this Jesus of yours really exists, then draw us a picture of him on the blackboard."

Maria thought for a moment before replying, "Yes, I can do that, but I'll need some golden chalk." The teachers were perplexed at this reply. They didn't have any golden chalk, so they let Maria go home.

Nina was a little older. She too belonged to Jesus' loyal young followers. Whenever the schoolchildren were told to do something that went against her conscience, she bravely stood on Jesus' side. As a result no one in the class would have anything to do with Nina; she was snubbed by everyone.

Someone stands beside me; His hand is always there.
As I hold it tightly, I'm assured of His care.
Jesus, O Love Everlasting.

One day the teacher tried to force her to carry the red flag at the head of a march. Nina refused. The teacher grabbed her by the arm and tried to shove the flag into her hand. But Nina firmly locked her arms behind her back. Next the teacher tried to stick the flag into the girl's jacket, but the flag fell to the ground. Infuriated, the teacher shouted at her, "This is an insult to the nation! You've shown contempt to the state! Why do you refuse to carry the red flag? Is it bloodstained or something?" Nina looked up and gazed into the angry eyes of her teacher and asked very quietly in return, "Why else is the flag so red?" Taken aback, the teacher fell silent and let Nina go.

So remember, the Lord Jesus will give each one of you the right answer at the right moment, just as He promised, if you belong to His loyal young followers. You may rely on this. Don't be afraid. For whatever the Lord Jesus promises He does for sure.

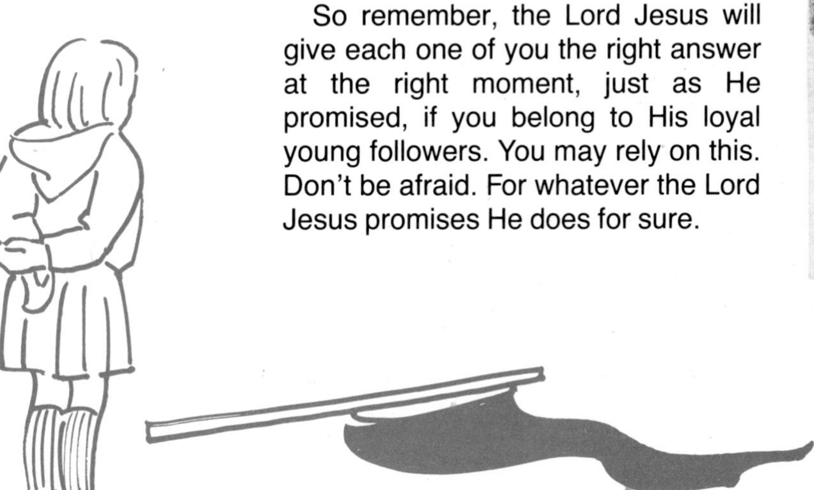

Jesus, dearest Lord, I pray,
Let me stay with You always.
I will never leave You.

What Made Them So Brave?

Where do you think these children found the courage to stand being ridiculed by their teachers, beaten up by their schoolmates and ignored by their class? Jesus gives us such courage when we ask Him for it. This goes especially for you children. Long ago when the Lord Jesus was on earth, God gave children courage when Jesus' enemies worked against Him and hated Him. One day when Jesus was in the Temple, in His Father's house, and surrounded by enemies, it was the children alone who showed great courage and welcomed Him with joy. Ignoring the anger of their religious teachers, they bravely took Jesus' side, singing songs of praise to Him, even though the scribes looked on with indignation (Matthew 21:15 & 16).

Again today when Jesus is attacked and rejected throughout the world, children will prove themselves as His loyal young followers. It could also happen in your class that a teacher says that there's no such thing as God, that you don't have to follow His commandments any longer, that it's old-fashioned to obey your parents, that there's nothing wrong with being rebellious, taking and saying what you please, or even doing indecent things. If you continue to believe in Jesus and take the commandments seriously and obey them instead of going along with the others, you might anger your teacher and turn the whole class against you.

If this happens, be glad and be proud of it! Now you can do just what the children did long ago when they shouted Hosannas to Jesus. You too can hail Him with joy and honour Him. Yes, you can be sure that Jesus will rejoice over His loyal young follower who sings His praises at the very time when everyone else is against Him.

Lord Jesus,
I'll stand up
for You
When
Your heart
is pierced
anew
By hatred's
bitter arrows.
I will live
and speak
for You –
God and
King
to whom
is due
All honour
and praise!

Lisa, What Happened? You Don't Stutter Any More!

Lisa lives in a country in the far north of Europe and had come to visit Canaan for a while. She is a living testimony of how Jesus can give us courage. Because she too is one of His loyal followers, she really wanted to testify to the Lord Jesus, whom she had come to love so dearly. But to give a testimony was twice as hard for Lisa as for any other child. Ever since she was a little girl, she had had a speech impediment and stuttered. But now all of a sudden her love for Jesus was greater than her fear. Lisa went to the headmaster of the school and asked whether she could say a word at the morning assembly in the large hall where all the teachers and children came together. And he gave her permission.

Think of what it would have been like if Lisa now began to stutter when she talked about Jesus! All seven hundred pupils would have roared with laughter! Every eye was fixed on Lisa as she walked up to the platform. But as she stood in front of the microphone and began to speak about Jesus, about her experience with Him and what He is like, it was most remarkable. For the first time in her life she could speak fluently. Her speech impediment was gone. Afterwards teachers and pupils came up to her and asked why she was suddenly able to speak without stuttering.

From this short story we see how Jesus cares for His loyal young followers. Whoever risks something for His sake and dares to stand up for Him, prepared at the same time to be made fun of for His sake will experience that Jesus draws near to him. He will know a joy and happiness that are far greater than the suffering he had to undergo.

O Jesus,
scorned as
never before,
Derided and
forsaken,
O Lamb of God,
beaten and
bruised,
Look now upon
Your children.
We want to go
with You,
O Lord,
Prepared to
suffer for You,
Your little
flock of
followers,
Who take their
stand
beside You.

Susie Has a Secret

Susie lives in a small German village. She is the youngest of five children and doesn't want to be outdone by her older brothers in anything. Though only five years old, she is like a little wildcat. Susie wriggles through the smallest holes, climbs over fences, rings doorbells. She kicks, scratches and bites. She is a real handful for her mother, and her little face is the picture of defiance. Whenever some of our Sisters stay for a while in our house there, they too have problems coping with the child.

But one day Susie was taken to see our small house chapel. There she saw the Lord Jesus hanging on a cross on the wall and she also saw Him as the Babe lying in a manger.

Susie stood still, deeply moved, and asked who it was. As she heard about Jesus, she said to the Sister, "You must take Him down from the wall. You must be nice to Him." The crucifix was taken down and placed before her.

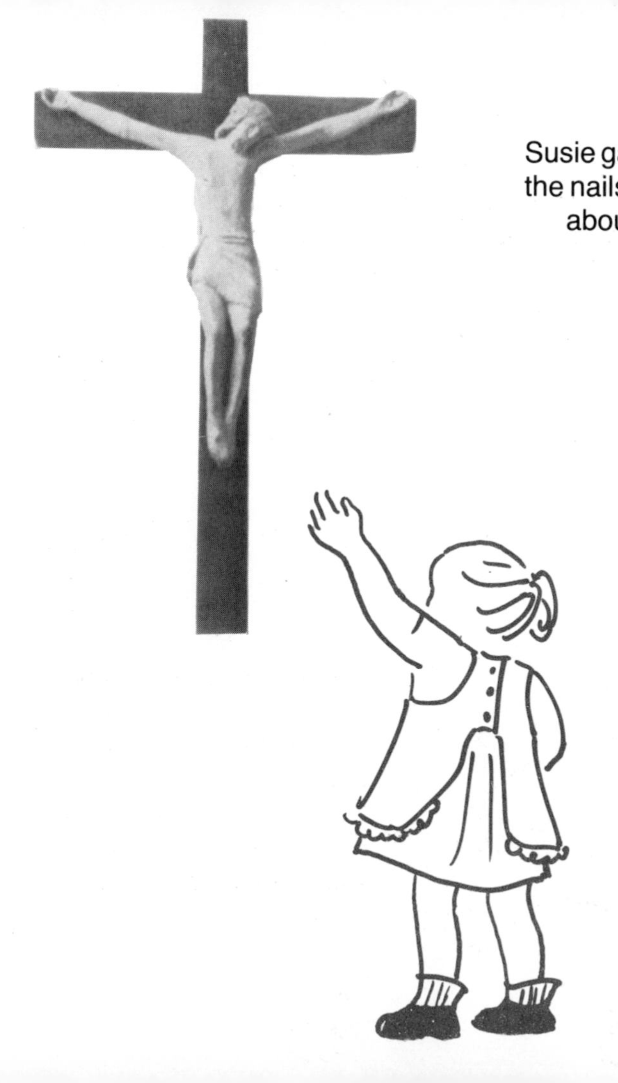

Susie gazed at it and then cried out, "You must take the nails out of Him right now!" She was very upset about the bad man who hammered the nails in. Then the Sister explained to Susie that for her sake too our Lord Jesus suffered such terrible pain and let the nails be driven through His hands and feet. Time and again we human beings are very wicked, but Jesus wants to free us from our wickedness.

From that time on there was a noticeable change in Susie's life.

2. He always
comes to help those
Jmprisoned
by sin.
O joy! He has
redeemed me;
J belong
now to Him.

3. Jn love He
reaches out now
To me, yes,
to me!
My chains move
Him to pity,
For a Saviour
is He!

4. My Saviour
truly came, J'm
As happy
as can be.
He loves me and
He saves me.
So J skip
joyfully.

Susie would have loved to take the crucifix with her – but, of course, that was not possible. And so now she comes to visit the Lord Jesus every day, bringing something along for the Baby Jesus in the manger and the Saviour on the cross – a bunch of flowers, her prettiest pictures and nicest playthings. And each time Susie first kneels down and sings the Baby Jesus "her song".

Susie is a different little girl now. From her face you can see that she knows how much the Lord Jesus loves her and that she yearns to love Him in return because of the great pain He suffered on the cross for us. When Susie calls at an inconvenient moment, she doesn't mind being sent away and asked to come later. Her mother says, "What has happened to Susie? She's become such a dear little girl, far more content and much happier." Before, she couldn't be naughty and wild enough, but now from the bottom of her heart she yearns to show the Lord Jesus all the love she can and not make Him sad again.

How the Lord Jesus must rejoice over Susie! How much her daily visit, her song, her prayers, her little presents must mean to Him! Children, think of how little love our Lord Jesus receives nowadays. All over the world people are disloyal to Him and are turning away from the Christian faith. They don't want to know anything more about God. They desert Him and grow more and more wicked as a result. That's why the world is filled with crime, terrorism and violence. In many families and homes there is no more peace. Strife, hatred and sin upon sin reign everywhere, making people utterly miserable, ruining their lives, and deeply hurting Jesus.

What must it mean to our Lord Jesus nowadays when children love Him, sing Him their songs and bring Him small presents of love! How much it must mean to Him when like Susie they stop doing the naughty things they wanted to do, thinking instead about what would please Him and what would hurt Him!

Do you see now? This is the kind of love that is prepared to suffer for our Lord Jesus when He is attacked. This is the love that always takes His side and defends Him as did Angela, Mike, Maria and Nina and many others who belong to His loyal young followers.

God's Little Land of Canaan and the Garden of Jesus' Sufferings

Before telling you about the Garden of Jesus' Sufferings, I first want to tell you where this garden is. You can find it in the little Land of Canaan, which is located on the outskirts of Darmstadt, a town in Germany (on the main road between Heidelberg and Frankfurt). For many years it was my heart's desire that the heavenly Father would give us this piece of land. We wanted to build on it and cultivate it and make it as beautiful as possible. It was to be a land where people would live in peace and love and reconciliation. In this land animals would be well cared for and feel as if they were in paradise. What a wonderful place that would be with beautiful flowers growing everywhere, flowing fountains, a bubbling brooklet and sunbeams dancing on a lake teeming with fish! All the visitors and all the people living at Canaan would come to love the Lord Jesus above all else. People would turn from their sins, and then be a living testimony throughout the world as to how happy God makes His children and how much He loves them.

The Lord worked many miracles and, in a wonderful way, He gave us this Land of Canaan, which we can now see before our eyes. If you want to hear how God did this and how He answers prayer nowadays, you can read all about it in the book "Realities – The Miracles of God Experienced Today"!

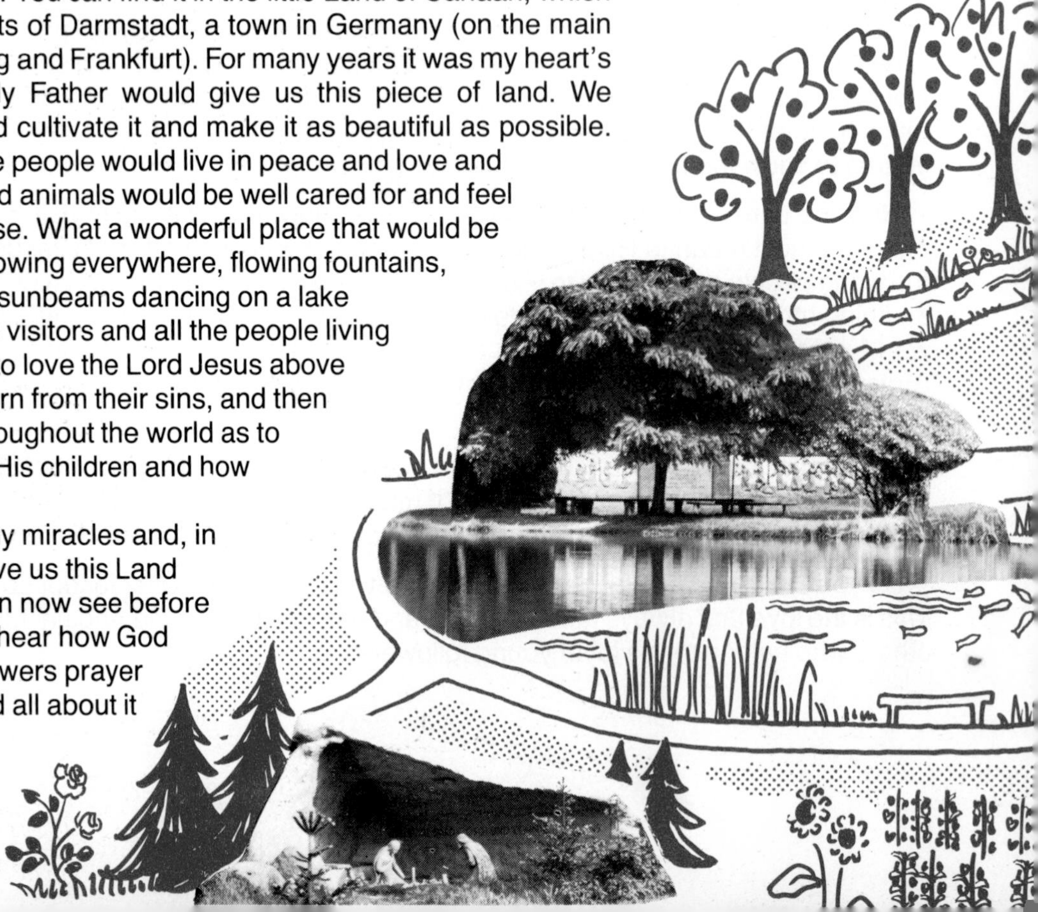

KANAAN

Joshua and Other Children in the Garden of Jesus' Sufferings

One day I said to Mother Martyria, "Let us thank the Lord Jesus for His bitter suffering by making a very lovely garden on the most beautiful part of our grounds, the area bordering the woods." And a garden really was made with gentle slopes and many shrubs, trees and flowers, quiet pathways and secluded spots for prayer. This is the Garden of Jesus' Sufferings. Stone monuments and sculptures show our Lord Jesus and His bitter suffering for us at different stages on His way to the cross. In this garden you can almost hear God's footsteps, for everything is wrapped in holy silence. The presence of Jesus is so real that you can almost breathe it. And once you are here, you don't want to go away any more. Many people travel a long way just to spend some time praying here. And you can well imagine the angels of God coming in the

evening to gather all the prayers – the words of thanksgiving and love, the songs, the tears shed over sin, the acts of dedication to suffering – and bringing them to the throne of God (Revelation 5:8). With these prayers from the Garden of Jesus' Sufferings the angels seek to bring a little comfort and joy to God's heart, which is greatly saddened by all the wickedness in our world.

When little Joshua from Africa came for a visit, he too didn't want to leave the Garden of Jesus' Sufferings. Though only three years old, he was deeply moved by the sufferings of our Lord Jesus. The Sister who took him there called him, because it was time to go, but Joshua couldn't bear to leave the garden. He stood crying and said, "I just have to keep looking at Him."

Why then? For the first time in his life little Joshua saw the Lord Jesus depicted in His sufferings. In the Grotto of Gethsemane Joshua saw our Saviour kneeling as He wrestled in prayer; no one was with Him. He saw Him being beaten and taken to court, tortured and ridiculed. He saw our Lord Jesus wearing a crown of thorns and sitting lonely on a rock. And there was no one who showed Him love or cared for Him. He saw our beloved Lord staggering beneath the heavy burden of the cross while wicked men pulled and prodded Him. He even saw children carrying nails and other tools for the crucifixion, although Jesus so dearly loved children. Cut to the heart by all the sufferings our Saviour endured for us, Joshua felt that he must love Jesus with all his might. And many other children have felt the same as Joshua down through the years.

Tom, for instance, a little American boy, was in his mother's arms as she walked through the Garden of Jesus' Sufferings with a large group of visitors. When they came to the place where the Lord Jesus is shown wearing a crown of thorns, Tom suddenly began to weep bitterly to see the Saviour looking so sad and lonely. Nothing could comfort the boy. The group, which had shown little response up till then, was now visibly moved. Because Tom wept out of love for Jesus, others were also affected – for love is always "contagious".

And there was eight-year-old Peter, who said to his mother after he had been in the Garden of Jesus' Sufferings, "I cried five times." He simply couldn't understand it that no one had ever told him about the Lord Jesus being beaten. "Why did He have to suffer so dreadfully?" We were able to tell him why, "For you and me – because of our sins."

In the Garden of Jesus' Sufferings you can soon spot the children who want to belong to His loyal young followers. They all love Jesus – and this is what binds them together.

Love always has a way of expressing itself. A boy once knelt down beside Jesus in Gethsemane, because he had read these words on the wall of the grotto:

"My Jesus, here will I kneel beside You at this rock of Your fear and agony. Out of love will I stay with You . . ."

At the place where Jesus is shown wearing a crown of thorns, a little child that couldn't reach high enough begged his mother to remove the crown of thorns, since "it pricks Him so much!" Others caress our Lord Jesus. They bring Him flowers and promise Him, "I will help You to carry Your cross." And others raise their fists threateningly at the wicked men who whip Jesus or put the cross upon Him, saying, "If only these men would leave the Lord Jesus alone for once!"

But Jesus probably rejoices most of all over those children who tell Him here that they now want to bear the things that are hard for them.

An older boy who was born with no arms, just hands, said with deep feeling, "The hand of the Lord Jesus is pierced by a nail, but how holy and mighty is the look on His face, not a bit furious or angry." This boy had understood the suffering love of Jesus, who doesn't lash out with angry words when His body is wounded. No, Jesus loves us so much that He willingly holds out His hands to bear wounds for our sake.

Perhaps you live so far away that you can't visit the Garden of Jesus' Sufferings and meet the other children who love the Lord and belong to His loyal young followers and who want to share His sufferings. But at least you now know that there are such children, and you know how much each one of them means to the Lord Jesus. He loves them. They are His pride and joy, His loyal subjects. Indeed, they belong to His small army. He will lead them into battle and gain the victory with them.

Our Lord Jesus knows that His loyal young followers want to be with Him at all costs and become like Him. They can't be separated from Him. They are willing to be hurt and bear suffering, since this will make them more like Jesus than anything else. Do you want to be one of His loyal followers too?

What Is Jesus' Most Beautiful Name?

Can you guess it after all that I've been telling you about the Garden of Jesus' Sufferings? In the Bible many names are given to the Lord Jesus. For instance, He is called KING, because He is mightier and greater than all the kings and rulers on earth. He is also called the GOOD SHEPHERD, because He cares for us like a shepherd for his little sheep. Other names of His are MIGHTY GOD and VICTOR, because He has defeated the devil. But for many His loveliest name is the LAMB OF GOD.

Have you ever seen a lamb? It is still young and weak and has a soft, white coat. It lets you do anything with it, not resisting when it is pushed this way or that.

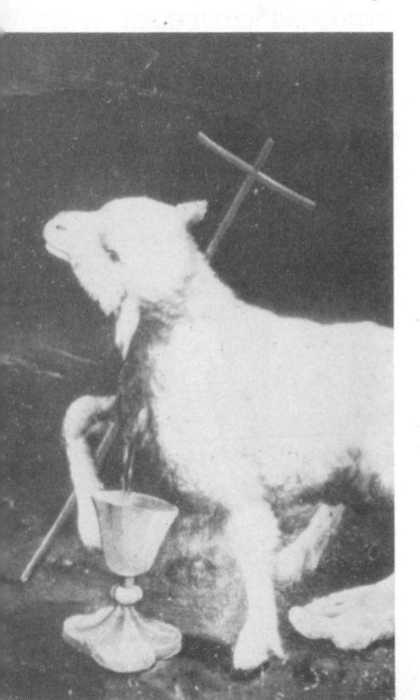

And since this is the nature of our Lord Jesus, the Bible often compares Him to a lamb. For although Jesus is the Lord of heaven and earth, He did not resist His tormentors and enemies on His way of suffering, nor did He ask His Father in heaven to destroy them. Of His own free will He took upon Himself the punishment that we deserve because of our wicked nature. Like a lamb He let Himself be dragged to and fro, pushed along and beaten and in the end allowed Himself to be nailed to the cross. This is why the name LAMB OF GOD is so beautiful; it helps us to see Jesus' great love for us.

The wonderful thing is that the Lord Jesus has redeemed us by His suffering, so that we too can be like a lamb – so meek and patient. You know that by nature we are often just the opposite, acting more like a bull or a mule. But if we want to belong

to our Lord Jesus, we really have to become a lamb. For only those who have been transformed into the image of Jesus will find the gates of heaven open to them one day. They will experience the tremendous joy of being with Him for ever and ever.

Take a look at the little lambs illustrated here. They all want to follow the Lord Jesus and be like Him, but something is not quite right with them. One of them has horns. It butts others and never wants to do the things it should do. Another one is wearing the crown of pride, because it thinks it is very important and always wants to be a somebody. And yet another one is lying down in a corner, defiant and refusing to co-operate. And a fourth is shown with a snake coming out of its mouth, because it so often says nasty, ugly words.

At the bottom of the page, there are some real little lambs. They are close to the Lord Jesus, the Lamb of God, and are following Him. They too used to have bad traits like the other lambs. But time and again they asked the Lord Jesus to forgive them and grant them His meek and patient, loving, lamblike nature. Now they can follow Him everywhere as His true little lambs and stay with Him even when the way is extremely hard. And we want to belong to them.

Steve Can Tell the Difference

It's Good Friday. The TV Guide said a film about Jesus would be shown. Ten-year-old Steve is very excited. Some time ago he had given his heart to the Lord Jesus and he regularly attends the children's classes that the Sisters hold in the "Jesus' Messenger Home". There you can see the Lord Jesus in a large picture made out of clay on the wall and hear the Sister tell about Him. How wonderful that is! – especially since there are so many sad things that we hear and see today.

On the television screen a man appears. He is supposed to be Jesus, but he looks and behaves like a hippy. Beat music is played the whole time. Steve is horrified and shouts, "Mother! Mother!" Then he bursts into tears. "That's not Jesus. The Sisters in 'Jesus' Messenger Home' have a completely different Jesus." Because Steve loves the Lord Jesus, he weeps bitterly and it is long past midnight before he can fall asleep. He is one of Jesus' loyal followers, as this little incident shows. This is why he can't bear to see such an ugly picture of Jesus and to think of Him being blasphemed in films and on television.

Dear children, many thousands may have seen this television show and yet they didn't cry. They couldn't tell the difference between the false Jesus and the true Jesus. Why not? Because they don't love Him. They may be important and rich and well-educated – and yet they didn't see anything wrong. But little Steve noticed the suffering of our Lord Jesus. He cried to see Him so degraded and with his tears he comforted his Lord. Love can always tell the difference. And Jesus will help you to do so. Then each one of you who belongs to Jesus' loyal young followers will be able to know when a false Jesus appears or is shown. Don't go to watch such things (Luke 17:23). Or as soon as you notice what it's all about, get up and go away. Then each time our Lord Jesus will see that you really belong to Him – and others will also see it – and some of them might begin to think and ask, "Who is this Jesus whom you love so much that you can't bear it when He is blasphemed and when a distorted image is shown of Him?"

Don't Be Afraid, Linda!

Linda lives in a big town, in a district where wicked things often happen. In the evening her father usually sits a long time in front of the television set and Linda watches with him. There she often sees programmes that frighten her so much that she can't even go to sleep afterwards. She also hears her parents talking about the violence, kidnapping and hostages they read of in the newspapers. Linda can't get rid of these thoughts. She's frightened.

One day Linda comes to Canaan. She is very quiet in order to take in everything about this new and different world. Suddenly Linda clasps the hand of the Sister and says, "Sister, you don't have any gangsters here, do you?" The Sister explains to her that the Lord Jesus and many angels live at Canaan. Her face beaming, Linda sighs deeply and sings to herself, "No gangsters, only angels! No gangsters, only angels!"

Before nightfall Linda is back home in "her world". She is still the same little girl, yet with a difference, for Jesus doesn't only live at Canaan or in a church. "I will be with you always" was His promise, and He even says in the Bible, "I know where you live." Now Linda can sing:

I rest in You, safe hidden, / O dearest Jesus mine. / When fears and cares surround me, / In You deep peace I find.

Within Your heart I'm resting, / Your love enfolds me there. /
Your heart knows all my suff'ring / And how much I can bear.

And this goes for each of you. Wherever you live and whatever your fears may be, greater still is the joy you will have as a child that loves and follows the Lord Jesus; you don't have to be afraid. In these days when fear and danger abound, you will find all the security and help you need in Jesus, the strongest Lord of all.

Jesus says to you and all the other children who belong to His loyal young followers:

"My child, I am
surrounding you on every side
and guarding you. And My angels
are round about you – mighty warriors,
who fight against gangsters
and everything else that frightens you."

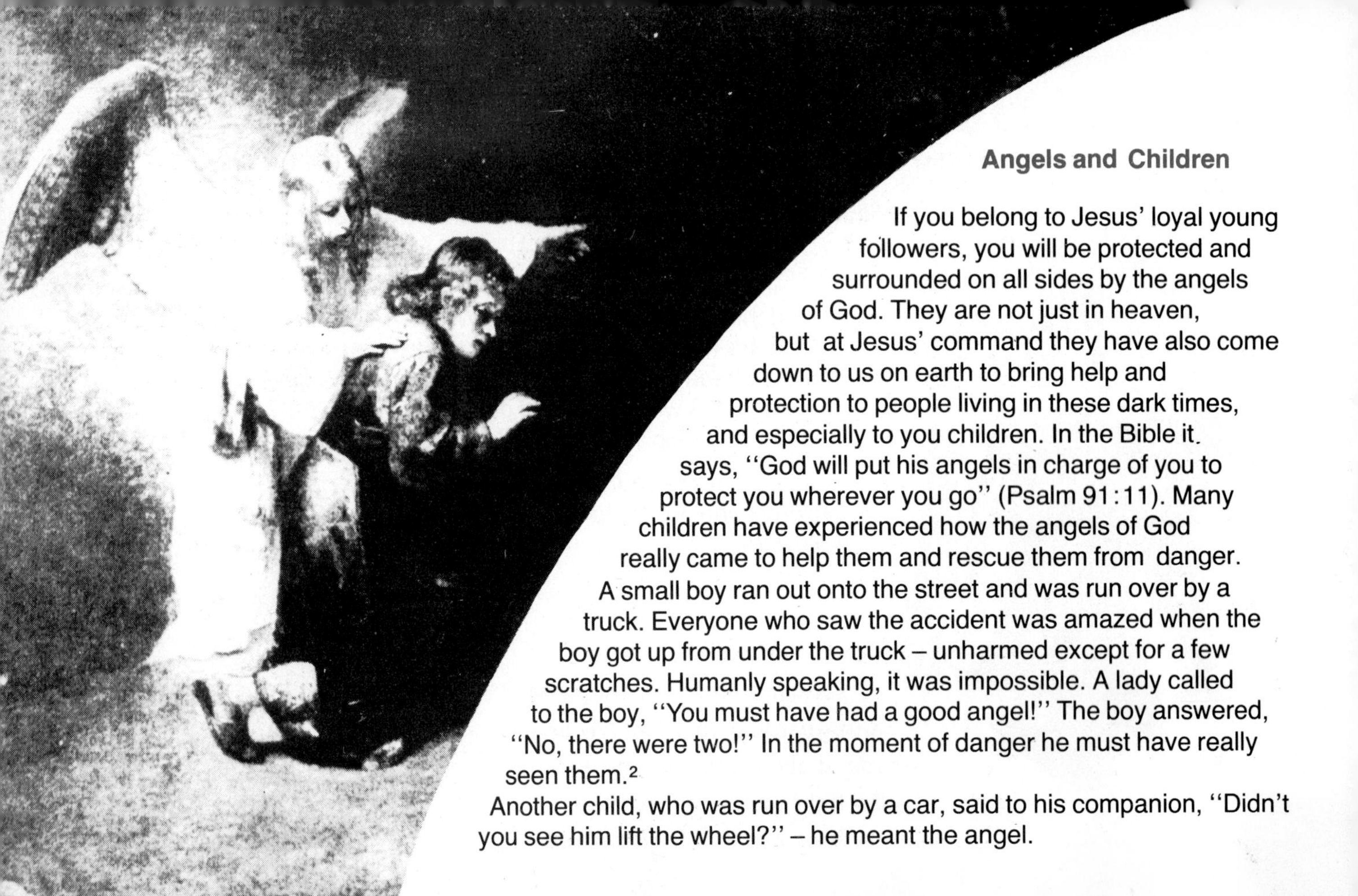

Angels and Children

If you belong to Jesus' loyal young followers, you will be protected and surrounded on all sides by the angels of God. They are not just in heaven, but at Jesus' command they have also come down to us on earth to bring help and protection to people living in these dark times, and especially to you children. In the Bible it says, "God will put his angels in charge of you to protect you wherever you go" (Psalm 91:11). Many children have experienced how the angels of God really came to help them and rescue them from danger.

A small boy ran out onto the street and was run over by a truck. Everyone who saw the accident was amazed when the boy got up from under the truck – unharmed except for a few scratches. Humanly speaking, it was impossible. A lady called to the boy, "You must have had a good angel!" The boy answered, "No, there were two!" In the moment of danger he must have really seen them.[2]

Another child, who was run over by a car, said to his companion, "Didn't you see him lift the wheel?" – he meant the angel.

There was a little girl whose father didn't believe in God. He said, "My child doesn't need a guardian angel!" But one day he happened to come home just as his little girl fell out of a window in the fourth storey. She should have been dashed to pieces on the pavement below. But the girl got up and rushed to her father, who shook his head in disbelief. "Daddy, I do have a guardian angel after all! Didn't you see him? I did. He was like a bright shining light and he carried me!"[3]

If the angels surround you children in everyday life, how much more will they protect you from the dangers for body and soul in these dark days at the end of time! Indeed, the heavenly Father's promise will come true, "His angel guards those who obey the Lord and rescues them from danger" (Psalm 34:7).

Whatever your name may be, wherever you may live and whoever you may be, Jesus and His angels love you. You are His child. For you He laid down His life. On the cross He suffered death, so that you may live in heaven for ever. And because He loves you so much, the Lord Jesus cannot but help you and send His angels when you are in distress. Count on this!

Cathy's Prayer for Help Is Answered

One day on the way to school Cathy had a terrible shock. A sinister-looking man tried to persuade her to go with him. In the end he pulled her into a lonely courtyard surrounded by ruins. Far and wide there was no one in sight. In her fear Cathy screamed, but then she called upon the Lord Jesus. When the man heard the child praying, he was suddenly prevented from carrying out his wicked plan. As if stunned, he let go of her and she was able to run away.

Believe that Jesus is present when you call upon Him – just as Angela experienced when, to the amazement and horror of her godless teacher, the Baby Jesus appeared. Of course, the Lord Jesus doesn't always reveal Himself in this manner. He is usually invisible, as in Cathy's case, but He is present indeed and always helps in some way, for He loves you so much.

Jesus makes only one condition. Do you know what that is? When He said that He is the Good Shepherd and that we – and especially you children – are His sheep, whom He leads in green pastures, whom He knows by name, loves and cares for, He added the words,

"My sheep listen to My voice, and they follow Me."

Lord, Your angels stand round me;
Let me nothing else now see
But these mighty warriors.
Let them keep watch o'er my heart.
Cast all fear and worry out;
Jesus, rule within me.

Jesus, You look after me
When J am in fear and need;
J can always trust You.
For Your own You ne'er forsake;
To Your heart Your child You take.
You are my true Refuge.

Our Lord Jesus always loves
Sad and fearful little ones,
Guarding them especially.
He'll watch o'er them day and night,
Strengthening them with His might.
Jesus mine, J trust You!

Which Voice Do You Listen To?

Hearing and obeying the right voice is not always easy in our times. Doubtlessly, some of you are still managing fairly well, because you have parents, teachers, Sunday school teachers and other grownups who love Jesus and help you. But often the situation is different, as you may have already discovered. Perhaps in a so-called Christian youth group or in religious instruction classes you are told that Jesus was a human being just like us, that He never was the Son of God, that He did not perform any miracles or supernatural deeds, and that the miracles reported in the Bible are fairy tales, etc.

When this happens, you must make up your mind which voice you are going to listen to and obey. Are you going to follow Jesus, who is alive, who performs miracles to this day and who is the Son of God? Or are you going to follow those who deny His existence and seek to lead you astray? You may be utterly bewildered and suddenly not know which voice is right, for after all it is your teacher, youth leader or even your parents, who are telling you such things. *Then what are you going to do?*

You may also be invited to Yoga classes; people may try to convince you that it's "just physical exercises". Or others may try to make TM sound especially appealing. But they don't tell you that these practices come from a pagan religion. In group discussions or certain classroom games you may be encouraged to tell others bluntly what you have against them. To see your own faults is said to be old-fashioned.

It could also be that in certain classes at school you hear statements such as: "If you obey, you are just like a slave." "You've got to be free and independent." "You have to learn to insist on your rights." "You can't simply obey your parents and those above you. They don't understand children anyway, and are just 'authority'." You may be encouraged to be rude towards grownups. Sometimes small handbooks are passed round teaching you anti-authoritarian behaviour. Other schoolchildren urge you to assert your rights as pupils to demand a say in the grading system and curriculum of the school. Your schoolmates go on strike. On all sides you are assailed by many voices. *Which one are you going to listen to?*

Or perhaps you have been told, "The commandments of God aren't meant for you. You are a different generation – you are young, modern people. The Bible is old-fashioned. It can't be applied to you nowadays!" Repeatedly you are told, "Jesus never demanded that you remain pure or live in obedience." The argument continues deceptively. "Jesus doesn't want you to be so legalistic. On the contrary, boys and girls were given these instincts to follow them. This is a perfectly natural part of your life. Only when you join in, will you find full satisfaction. Otherwise you are immature and prudish." And in sex education classes you may be urged to do indecent things. Even the youngest ones of you may be taken to the most disgusting shows and made to imitate the things you see and do things to one another that you are actually ashamed to do. According to God's commandments such things are a serious sin, but suddenly you are told that they are proper and right.
Which voice are you going to listen to now?

Call upon Me in Your Troubles

When the voices of temptation draw near you, the first thing you should do is to call. Call again and again, "Come, Lord Jesus!" – and you will experience that He is alive. Angela's teacher tried to prove to the children that Jesus was dead, but instead Jesus proved that He was alive. When teachers and other grownups try to tell you today that you don't have to keep the commandments of God any longer, they are saying exactly the same thing, "Jesus isn't alive. He is not the Son of God, nor is He your Good Shepherd. He is not with you and doesn't love you."

Don't believe them and don't let them lead you astray. Rather call all the more to God and He will answer you in His good time. Recently someone told me that in another country children were cruelly taken away from their Christian parents in order to be "re-educated". These poor children, most of whom were believers, were taken far away to a small town. There, completely cut off from their parents, they were put under godless teachers. Not only the parents at home, but also the children cried to God day and night, that He might help and deliver them. They didn't want to listen to these godless teachers who tried to mislead them. They wanted to remain loyal to Jesus. And what happened?

One day there was suddenly a great commotion. Something was written in the sky. It said, "Lo, I am coming soon." Many saw it, and even the traffic came to a standstill. Terror seized the teachers and the others who were trying to re-educate the children and turn them away from God. For from the words in the sky everyone was forced to see that God was alive after all and that Jesus would come again. The school was closed down and the children were returned to their parents. This is what our God is like! The Lord Jesus and the Father in heaven help us when we cry to Them in the deepest distress!

The point is, you must really call upon the Lord – not just once, but ever anew. Don't listen to the voices of those who try to lead you astray. Do not pay any attention to them. Don't think about what they say and don't let their words enter your hearts. Otherwise you will lose not only a little of what you have, but everything. For these people who are trying to mislead you deny everything that the Bible says about Jesus; they want to destroy your belief in those eternal truths, which are meant for you personally:

- The Lord Jesus will be coming soon on the clouds of heaven with power and great glory.
- He is your Judge, to whom you must one day give account for all that you have said and done, and He will judge you accordingly.
- After you die, Jesus will either open the gates of heaven for you, where you will be happy for ever and have no more sorrows,
- or else He will allow the gates to the kingdom of darkness and agony to be opened, where Satan, its ruler, will torment you.

Those who led others astray will one day end up in this terrible kingdom of the devil and his servants. But Jesus wants you who belong to His loyal young followers to be close at His side in the heavenly glory. And such a goal is worth every struggle today.

When these deceiving voices try to rob you of everything that you know about Jesus and spoil every experience that you may have had with Him, when you're torn by questions and doubts, the Bible has a word of advice and a sure promise for you in your troubles:

"When you call to me, I will respond"
(Isaiah 58:9).

When you ask Jesus, "What is the truth?", He will answer you, "I am the Truth. I will tell you the truth. And you will know the truth."

The truth is: You are to live pure lives. Children, obey your parents, honour them and those placed above you. The truth is that whoever listens to His commandments and does them will be happy and heaven will open to him. For as it is written in Holy Scripture, blessed are those who do His commandments – they shall enter the gates of the City of God (Revelation 22:14).

On the other hand, remember that what the other voices say to you comes from Satan, the father of lies, the foe of Jesus Christ and mankind. He and the demons, who belong to his kingdom, are a reality – even if clever people say they are just spooks and that it is ridiculous to believe in their existence. Today more than ever these demons are at work, struggling to trap each one of us. They constantly try to lure you into doing wicked deeds and make sin seem pleasant to you, only to torment you afterwards. But disobedience remains sin. To do indecent things is sin. Lying is sin. And sin is something terrible. It destroys the soul, the spirit and the body. It has frightening effects and in the end, if we do not repent and bring our sins to Jesus, we shall fall into Satan's clutches for ever.

We trust, Lord, Your victorious power!
You speak, and all obey.
At Your name, O Jesus, the demons turn and run away.

Eric and the Herald Play

In our Land of Canaan you can see the large Herald Chapel. Several times a year on certain afternoons crowds of people come from far and wide to see a Herald Play. When the bell in the steeple has been rung, and when all is dark and very quiet inside the chapel, the spotlight begins to shine on the altar in the front. On the wall behind the altar is a picture of our Lord Jesus as the Lamb of God. Angels enter and sing glorious songs about His beauty and splendour. On the lower chancel steps, scenes from everyday life are enacted. All of a sudden evil spirits, demons, appear and try to lead the people astray. But the voice of God fills the whole chapel and says what the right way is. The holy angels also join in the battle, so that many souls will be saved and find their way back to God.

Strictly speaking, these Herald Plays are only for grownups. Children can play on the grounds of Canaan during the performance. But Eric, who is also one of Jesus' young followers, thought he just had to see the Herald Play, which the grownups talked about so much. He slipped inside and begged one of the Sisters to let him stay. He just had to see it! Since he was only seven years old, the Sister thought he wouldn't be able to sit still for long. So she took him on her lap, thinking she could later take him out to the other children when it became too much for him.

But Eric was as quiet as a mouse. He saw the shining angels. He heard them singing and calling to the people who were talking to each other on the steps below the altar. All of a sudden a group of demons rushed in. There on the lower steps they unfolded a fiendish plot to ensnare all the people they had not yet led astray. The devils were sure of victory.

The head devil shouted, "Let's take a look at the way things are going. We don't have much more time. We've already accomplished the greater part of our plans. Most people are separated from God. They either hate him or they have forgotten all about him. The commandments are no longer taken seriously. No one wants to hear the word 'sin' any more. Authority is no longer respected. Terror and violence are ruling the earth. Many Christians are sleeping and a good number of them have been won over to our side. Our slogan for the last round is: Use every minute!"

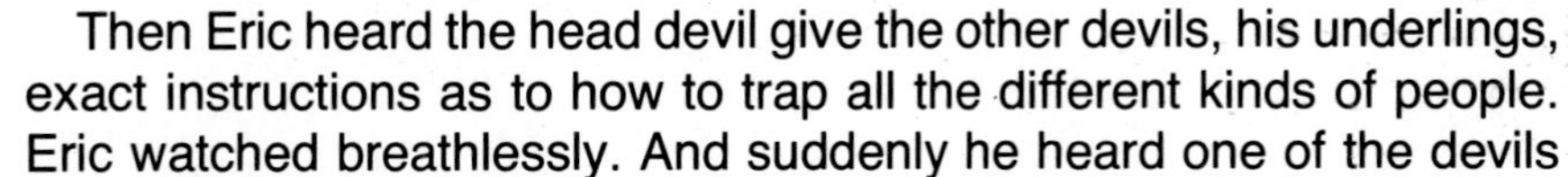

Then Eric heard the head devil give the other devils, his underlings, exact instructions as to how to trap all the different kinds of people. Eric watched breathlessly. And suddenly he heard one of the devils say, "I'll put sex in films, on television, in magazines, on radio, on the stage. Even children will be fed with sex!" At this Eric, who was leaning forward, completely enthralled by the play, sat up straight and shouted, "But he won't get me!"

Resist the Devil!

Be like Eric. Remember, Jesus is stronger than the devil and all his demons taken together. If you belong to Jesus, He will fight for you and beat the devil every single time.

Don't listen to the devil's voice or to human voices that seek to lead you astray. Resist them instead. The Bible says, "Resist the devil and he will flee from you" (James 4:7 RSV). Let him see that your mind is really made up. If you begin to pay attention to deceptive voices and let them into your heart because you find them appealing or if you let the demons have their say, you are in the danger zone. Soon they will have you.

But if you stand against them in the name of God, just as young David stood against the giant Goliath (1 Samuel 17:45), Satan cannot harm you. You can call upon the name of Jesus and hurl this name against the devil, just as David slung his smooth stones. Whenever you hear the voices of temptation, say:

"In the name of Jesus, go away!
I don't want to have anything to do with you.
Jesus is Victor!"

Then you will experience that they are put to flight. You will be victorious, and peace and joy will fill your heart every time the devil is driven back.

But it would be terrible if you listened to these voices of deception and did what they said. Children who do so are attacked by the demons and tormented by them. They suffer from fear. Many can no longer sleep at night. They can scarcely laugh or be happy. At school they are unable to cope with the work. It's as though they have been caught in a web. To carry on their sinful habits, they need money. To obtain the money, they steal, and when they have stolen, they cover up their deed with lies. When punished at home, they run away. And since they no longer know the meaning of true joy, they turn to sinful pleasure. But their lust gets the better of them and they can't control it – the flames are fanned into a fire that they can't put out. Many children have caught terrible diseases by committing sexual sins. And others have to go to a psychiatrist for treatment, because they are emotionally disturbed. In other cases children drink alcohol or take drugs to escape from reality, and in the process they fall desperately ill and some even die.

This avalanche was set going when they listened to the voices of deception. But Satan has no pity at all for them; he has achieved his objective – to plunge them into misery. So I repeat, "Resist the devil and he will flee from you!"

If the Tempter, Satan, or wicked spirits or human beings try to convince you that disobedience, rebelliousness and impurity are right, then begin to pray! In prayer there is power to put the Enemy to flight. So pray:

JESUS,
forgive me and
wash my sins
away by Your blood,
so that You can
come to me
again.

JESUS
is Victor!

JESUS,
I will take Your hand,
for You are my
Good Shepherd,
who always
guides
me.

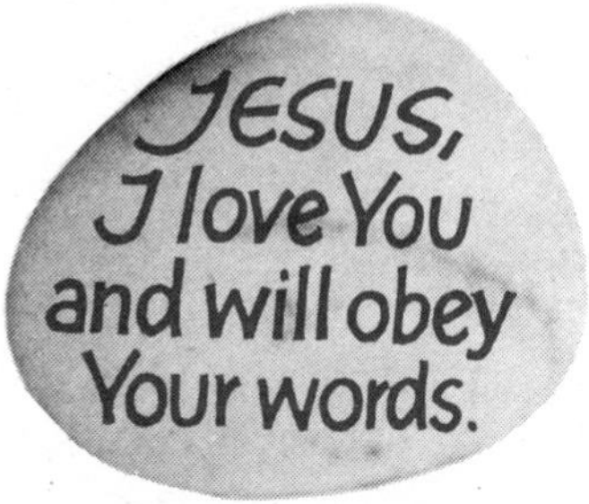

JESUS,
I love You
and will obey
Your words.

JESUS, under the protection of Your blood I am safe, and Satan must flee.

JESUS, I want to be Yours and never leave You, I want to stay on Your pathway.

JESUS, I want to remain faithful to You – come what may, I will cling to You.

JESUS, grant that I may never lose this one thing – heaven, my eternal home.

These short prayers are just as effective as the smooth stones that David hurled against the giant Goliath. The Enemy will be overcome and forced to let you go. For the name of Jesus is the greatest power and the strongest weapon of all.

If you keep on hearing the voice of the Tempter, then say like Eric, "But he won't get me!" Look to the commandments of God for answers, guidance and advice in making decisions. They are the only signposts along the road that will not lead you astray.

Don't listen to anyone who says something different from what Jesus or the Bible says. Jesus, whose words are always valid, is the only authority that will remain for ever and before whom we must all appear one day. He will then ask us about all that we have done here on earth and judge us accordingly.

However honoured and respected a person may be, don't treat him as the highest authority if he tries to make you do bad things. God is the highest authority. And if something goes against your conscience, don't do it, even if it's your parents or teachers who are telling you to. Obey Jesus and His commandments, and you will be a happy child and heaven will be yours. In the Bible God says that by giving us the commandments He gives us a choice. We can either choose life and happiness, that is, peace and joy, by keeping the commandments, or death and unhappiness by not keeping them (Deuteronomy 30:15ff.).

I once looked up the commandments of God, which can be found throughout the Bible,and wrote them down in a book. It is called "More Precious than Gold". As I did so, my heart was filled with ever-increasing gratitude that God in His great love gave us the commandments as signposts, which clearly show us the way in every situation in our lives. So whenever many voices of temptation are harassing you, pray to God for an answer from the Bible, from His commandments. Then you will experience what I have experienced so often: God still speaks today. And you can be sure that whoever does His commandments will not only be the happier for it, but as the Bible says he will be wiser than others. This is not surprising, for he is doing the will of God and God is the wisest of all. This is why the Psalmist says:

Therefore I love thy commandments above gold, above fine gold.
Thy commandments are my delight.
Thy word is a lamp to my feet and a light to my path.
The law of thy mouth is better to me than thousands
of gold and silver pieces.
I will run in the way of thy commandments.
They are the joy of my heart.

Children who love the commandments of God and keep them will never fall prey to the devil. Rather they will be a joy to God and all the angels in heaven.

A Pure Heart – But How?

"You are always saying I should steer clear of all filth," complained John one day, "But what should I do when I hear so many dirty things? The other children tell dirty jokes. There is so much filth in school classes, films, books and television shows. The very air is filthy – and yet I've still got to breathe!"

Perhaps you feel just like John and have no one you can talk things over with. But remember, you have a special privilege – you may talk everything over with Jesus. Go to Him quickly and say, "My Lord Jesus, speak to me, for I want to obey Your voice."

You may bring Him all your questions in prayer: "Lord Jesus, I can't manage to close my ears and keep my eyes shut all the time. Can You help me?" Perhaps the Lord Jesus will say, "Shut your eyes, close your ears, and even if you are laughed at and scolded, be a brave young soldier and bear wounds willingly for Me. Look at Me and think of how I was whipped long ago and of the blood that flowed from My many wounds for Your sake. This blood will cleanse you when you often hear or see dirty things without meaning to. It will also cleanse you when it is your fault and you are very sorry for having had dirty thoughts and feelings."

Yes, the blood of Jesus washes away every sin if you bring it to Him. Confess these sins to your parents, or, if they are not Christians, to another grownup who is a Christian.

Do you do everything in your power to keep away from bad things? For instance, do you avoid looking at filthy or gruesome things on television or in books and magazines? When all the other children boast of having seen the most gory thrillers or indecent films on television, be brave and openly admit that you have not watched them because you didn't want to. When you are at home or at your friends' homes, don't be lured into watching TV. There are so many nice things you could do instead that would bring joy to the Lord Jesus and yourself. And when you go past the newsstand or the billboard with film advertisements on the way to school, look the other way and think about the Lord Jesus. Pray every day:

Create in me a pure heart.
Shut out all filth and sin,
And drive away all wickedness.
Don't let them stay within.

To You my heart I open.
O Jesus, dwell in me,
And cleanse me, Lord, Your temple,
Of all impurity.

Remember, only if you have a pure heart and have led a pure life, will you be fit for heaven. Only children – and for that matter, grownups too – who by the power of Jesus' redemption have become as transparent as glass and as pure as heaven with no trace of filth on them may dwell with Jesus in His heavenly glory. And this is where He is waiting for you!

These Wicked Times Won't Last Long

Have you ever thought or said, "Dear Lord Jesus, it's awful having to live at a time like this. What will come of it all? Why is it that nowadays most people, including children, call things good and right that You have said are not right, but bad and wicked? I just don't understand it."

While on earth, the Lord Jesus foretold a time that would come, which He called the "close of the age". He described what it would be like and said this period would be short. It is a time when all over the world wickedness and goodness will come to full maturity and good and bad alike will ripen like fruit. He also said that the good would be only small in number – and they would be His loyal followers. But wonderful things are in store for them.

True, the world is dark today and will grow even darker. The devil is now celebrating his triumph and every form of iniquity abounds. The wicked boast and think they have all the power. What they say must be done. And whoever refuses will have to pay for it. They talk about peace, but create chaos everywhere, turning the world into hell.

But you know, children, that won't last very much longer. During this "age of lawlessness" when God and His commandments are hated, our Lord Jesus Christ will suddenly come again in great power and glory – visible to all. He will then judge those who were wicked and did not repent of their sins. He will judge those who did indecent things and those who rebelled. He will judge the terrorists, the vandals, the liars and criminals. But what will happen to His loyal followers?

JESUS IS COMING! Just imagine! Jesus will appear in His royal might and beauty as the heavenly Bridegroom to all who love Him. In great love He will gather them to Himself and bring them into heaven amid the singing and rejoicing of all the angels. If you love the Lord Jesus above everything else and belong to His loyal followers, you will be there too. Then you will skip and sing for sheer joy and think you are dreaming. All this awaits you.

Wonderful it must be / High in eternity, /
Close by the Father and Holy Spirit / And angels gathered round.

O might J soon be there / Where music fills the air, /
Angels in heav'n are endlessly praising; /J too shall worship You.

KD No. 24

Heaven Is Yours!

Perhaps others make fun of you and laugh at you. You may feel all alone at school or the children in your neighbourhood may turn their backs on you – and all because you are bravely standing on Jesus' side. But one thing is sure: heaven is open to Jesus' loyal young followers.

What a wonderful word!
Heaven – the place where Jesus lives!
Heaven – where He will gaze at you, His face radiant with immeasurable love and beauty!
Heaven – where Jesus will take you into His arms in great joy!

Heaven, where the angels move in gracious dance and sing the most glorious songs as they lead you into a world of dazzling light and beauty and overwhelming joy, is open to you not only in the future but right now. If you follow Jesus, heaven will come down to you. And you will taste the joy of heaven, especially when you suffer for Him.

Jesus saved you, so that you could have a foretaste of heaven even now in the midst of suffering. He saved you, so that heaven and not the kingdom of darkness would be your home at the end of your life. So rejoice, heaven is yours. You are heading towards heaven. Say:

> "Jesus has prepared a home in heaven for me. After this short time on earth I shall be with Him for ever in heaven – yes, for all eternity. That is my home and no one can take it away from me. And even now, my Lord Jesus, You come to me as the days grow darker and more difficult to bear."

My heart sings with gladness,
with joy - and love, / For Jesus
prepares - my home there a-bove. /
A wonder-ful home for e-

ter - ni - ty. / J know my dear

Saviour prepares it for me.

KD No. 29

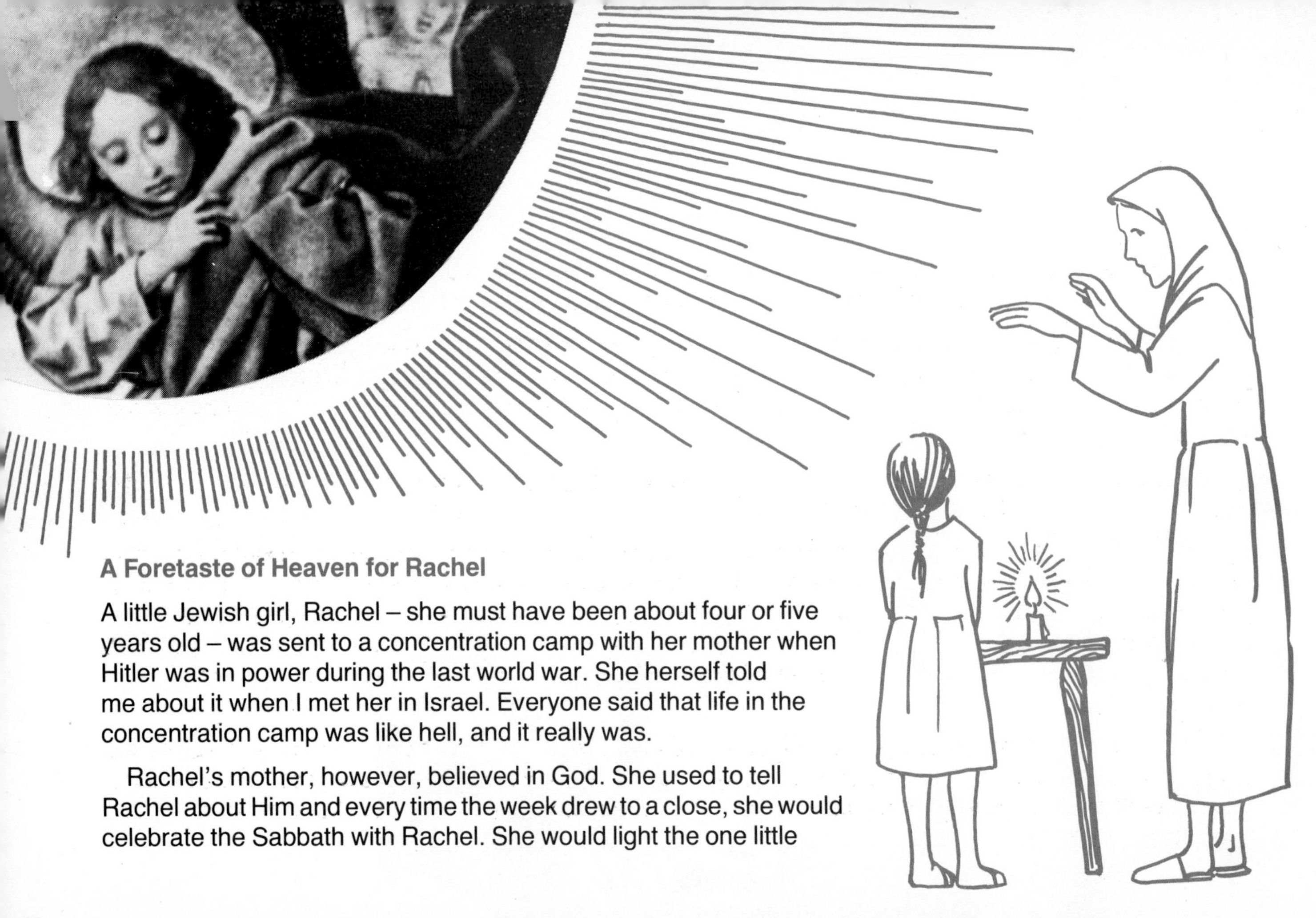

A Foretaste of Heaven for Rachel

A little Jewish girl, Rachel – she must have been about four or five years old – was sent to a concentration camp with her mother when Hitler was in power during the last world war. She herself told me about it when I met her in Israel. Everyone said that life in the concentration camp was like hell, and it really was.

Rachel's mother, however, believed in God. She used to tell Rachel about Him and every time the week drew to a close, she would celebrate the Sabbath with Rachel. She would light the one little candle she possessed and pray with Rachel her favourite prayers. At these times God was so close that it seemed as if heaven had come down. Shortly before they were to be killed, they were rescued.

Later when Rachel was grown up and married in the United States, she once said to her mother with tears in her eyes that her life had never been so happy as it was during her childhood when her mother prayed and celebrated the Sabbath with her in the concentration camp. She had had a real experience of heaven then.

You see, children, the hunger pangs, the fears, the terrors, yes, even the threat of death faded into the background for Rachel, because God and the heavenly world drew so near.

And so you don't need to be afraid when you hear of Christians being persecuted nowadays in other countries and when persecution threatens all who belong to Jesus' loyal followers. Your heavenly Father is the very best father there is. He cares for His children, just as we read in the Bible about David. When he was persecuted, he came to know the Father and His ways, and so he could rejoice and, filled with praise, write in one of his psalms, "You are all round me on every side; you protect me with your power" (Psalm 139:5).

Trust, and you will find that the Lord Jesus is present. He will come to you and help you, as He did Angela, Mike, Maria and Nina and all His loyal young followers. He will drive away your fear, as He did for Linda and Rachel. He will wrap you in His love, just as a mother hen spreads out her wings protectingly over her baby chicks.

His Loyal Young Followers

Right now when so many voices are trying to make you rebel against God, against our Lord Jesus, a challenge is being made to you children. It is the challenge to stand on His side, to say you belong to Him, to fight for Him – and even bear wounds for His sake. Often these are not bodily wounds that can be seen, but wounds in the heart that hurt just as much – especially those caused by ridicule. Such wounds are an honour for you to bear. They make you more like our Lord Jesus, who was so cruelly beaten and bore these wounds because of our sins. We should love our Lord Jesus very dearly, seeing that He suffered so much for us.

But perhaps you say, "To be persecuted by wicked people and God-haters is a terrible thing. And suffering remains suffering even when Jesus is near. Will I really be able to endure it?"

Yes, if you are faithful to Jesus in all the small sufferings of today, if you take His side and follow Him, you will be able to be steadfast in the greater sufferings of tomorrow. And not only will you be able to endure, but you will count it a privilege to suffer for Jesus.

Mark, a ten-year-old boy living in Eastern Europe, asked a visitor from a country in the West, "What are you suffering for Jesus?"

For Mark it was quite natural to think that if this visitor was a Christian he would be suffering for Jesus. Mark had been separated from his parents. They were thrown into prison for witnessing to Jesus, and Mark himself was sent to a camp with the purpose to make him lose his faith in God. But when he was released from the camp, he had an even stronger faith in God. Suffering for Jesus had made him strong and happy and brought him spiritual blessings. In this time of great distress he came to know Jesus and the reality of heaven as never before. And for this reason he thought it only an honour to suffer for such a wonderful Lord, for Jesus, the Son of God and King of kings.[4] Indeed, this is the greatest honour we can ever have.

And on the following pages I would like to tell you some more about this. You will find the next story very encouraging.

The Most Pitiable Cripple, But the Most Beautiful Christian

Not long ago a Chinese Christian paid us a visit. For many years he had been living outside of his native land as a refugee. But recently he had a chance to revisit his homeland. During the past years in China, the Christians have been cruelly persecuted and many of them killed. Those who were still alive had all been through great suffering and were now radiant witnesses for Jesus – a fact that deeply moved our Chinese friend. Then he told us about a boy who was one of Jesus' loyal young followers:

"I met Daniel, a crippled boy, in a town in southern China. He hadn't always been a cripple, but he will remain a cripple for the rest of his life. Daniel told me his story. 'During the Cultural Revolution, which began in 1966, Mao was made into the "god" of China. Mao was "god" – everyone was forced to worship him.' In Daniel's village everyone had to kneel and bow down before Mao's picture – in the morning, at midday, and in the evening before going to bed. But Daniel refused to kneel down before Mao. He said, 'I will not kneel down before him, because I am a Christian.'

"The Red Guard in the village then tried to force him to kneel, but again he refused. At that the young revolutionaries brought Daniel to their leader, who called a people's court. Everyone in the village was assembled in the market place and the leader conducted the trial. He ordered the young Christian to kneel and bow down before Mao's picture, or else . . . ! But Daniel refused again. The leader of the Red Guard flew into a rage. He felt disgraced before the entire village. And seeing that Daniel persisted in his attitude, he ordered the Red Guard to break the boy's legs, so that he would lie on his bleeding knees before Mao's picture. Daniel fainted from the terrible pain. He was then taken to a labour camp. But he never denied Jesus.

"When I saw Daniel, he told me, 'Brother, they broke my legs, but they couldn't break my faith.' What a great love Daniel had for Jesus! He was the most pitiable cripple that I had ever seen, but also the most beautiful Christian. Jesus shines in his face. Jesus is his King. And people can see this simply by looking at him."

From this deeply moving story about Daniel you see that God doesn't always come to save us from great suffering as He did in the lives of the many other children mentioned earlier on. But you can also see that the heavenly Father makes true another of His promises written in the Bible – especially in times of suffering – He never lets us be tempted beyond our strength. When He lets us go through great suffering, He increases our strength to bear it and in the midst of suffering He increases our joy and love for Jesus. He will then be very close to us and His great power will be in us, just as Daniel and Rachel and Mark experienced. But how much more will the Lord reward one day in heaven those of you who have suffered for His sake! This will surpass all that we could ever imagine or expect!

Thou knowest
I am weak and small;
I cannot bear such pain at all.
How quickly I'd lose courage!
And yet I can do everything
When Thou dost touch and strengthen me;
Then I am strong, courageous. FT No. 18

The greatest gift that the Lord Jesus can grant to all those who love Him and who are faithful to Him is the privilege of living in heaven. They are to dwell in the Golden City one day. The Bible calls it "the heavenly Jerusalem" and God Himself has built it.

This city sparkles like precious jewels. It has a high wall with twelve gates and at each gate is a mighty, shining angel. The streets are paved with pure gold, transparent as glass. From the heart of the city flows a river as clear as crystal and trees grow on its banks, bearing very special fruit twelve times a year. Whoever eats the fruit becomes happy and healthy. This city needs neither sun nor moon nor lamps, for the Lord Jesus lives there, shining with greater radiance than a thousand suns.

There the Lord is waiting for you, His loyal young followers, who fight for Him in His army, suffering for His sake as brave soldiers, some of you even laying down your lives as martyrs. Jesus, our King, will crown you with a wonderful crown. He will lift you up to His throne and present you with pride to all the heavenly hosts. Then you will be able to stay at His side for ever. With Him you will ride through the heavens on white horses and rejoice in heavenly pastures.

Let us press onward bravely
And to the throne be looking.
As great the pain, so bright the crown.
Let's pay no heed to suff'ring,
But live with joyous yearning
For that great day when we return home.

And so we would bear suff'ring;
It helps prepare great glory,
The likes of which have ne'er been seen.
Our goal – the throne of splendour,
To dwell with God for ever,
Where time and suff'ring will be no more.

FT No.23

So be willing to suffer as a brave soldier of Christ Jesus
and one day you will inherit the crown of life.
Surrender your life fully to Jesus in love, for He loves
you so much. It's worth sharing His way as
His loyal young follower.

Close to Your heart, dear Jesus,
Your child would ever stay,
For when I'm in Your keeping,
All sorrow melts away.
You know what I can bear, Lord,
In my great frailty.
You weigh my daily burden
And Your arms cradle me.

Prayer before Beginning a New Day at School

My dear Lord Jesus,

Before this new day at school begins, I take hold of Your hand. I want to follow You today. I want to stay on Your pathway, obeying You and Your commandments, so that You can protect me in all that happens today and guide me along Your paths.

I trust You and know that You won't leave me, for You have promised,

"Do not be afraid; I am with you."

If I am tempted today, if I hear a deceiving voice and am in danger of agreeing to do something bad, let me remember that You are watching me and waiting to see whether I will now prove my love to You, take Your side, and do what You have said.

Help me to make the right decision in each situation, so that I behave just as You have told me in the Bible and just as my conscience tells me.

I want to follow You, because You love me so dearly and because You have suffered so much for me. Yes, I want to be faithful to You, even if others make fun of me and hurt me. I want to be Your loyal follower who fights on Your behalf.

You will give me the courage for this by Your precious blood. I trust You, my Lord Jesus. You are my Helper, the mighty Prince of victory!

Amen.

Song References

page 9	NJ = taken from M. Basilea Schlink, IN THE NAME OF JESUS, prayers and songs for the battle of faith (American edition: SONGS AND PRAYERS OF VICTORY)
page 20	WJ = taken from WELL-SPRING OF JOY, songs of the Sisters of Mary for singing or praying
pages 59, 61	KD = taken from M. Basilea Schlink, THE KING DRAWS NEAR, songs about Jesus' second coming and the heavenly glory
pages 68, 69, 72	FT = taken from M. Basilea Schlink, MY FATHER, I TRUST YOU, songs of trust and dedication

Credits

1. pp. 6–7	based on Maria Winowska, DIE IKONE, TATSACHEN AUS DER KIRCHE DES SCHWEIGENS (Paulusverlag, Freiburg, Switzerland, 1960)
2. p. 36	based on Wilhelm Horkel, BOTSCHAFT VON DRÜBEN (Moritz Schauenburg Verlag, Lahr, West Germany, 1975)
3. p. 37	based on A. M. Weigl, IN GOTTES VATERHAND (Verlag St. Grignionhaus, Altötting, West Germany, 1971)
4. p. 65	based on DER CHRISTUSBOTE (Remscheid, West Germany – Rundbrief March/April, 1973)

Picture Credits

Reprints by kind permission:

cover photo, pp. 13, 15, 57	Fra Angelico, The Risen Lord – Wilhelm Schamoni, DAS LEBEN UNSERES HERRN CHRISTUS (Kreuzring Bücherei, Johannes-Verlag, Leutesdorf, West Germany)
p. 7	Fra Angelico, Child Jesus with Orb (Buch-Kunstverlag Ettal, West Germany, 508)
p. 9	Rudolf Schäfer, Blessing the Children – STUTTGARTER BILDERBIBEL (Deutsche Bibelstiftung Stuttgart, West Germany, 1955)
p. 30	Matthias Grünewald, Lamb of God, Isenheim Altar – Musée d'Unterlinden, Société Schongauer, Colmar, France
pp. 34, 35, 71	Fra Angelico, Angels Making Music (Riproduzioni artistiche S.R.L. Roberto Hoesch, Milan, Italy)
p. 36	Rembrandt, Daniel's Vision at the River Ulai – DIE BIBEL IN DER KUNST, DAS ALTE TESTAMENT (Phaidon Press LTD, London, England, 1957)
pp. 40, 41	Michael Pacher, Detail from The Temptation of Christ – Eberhard Hempel, DAS WERK MICHAEL PACHERS (Verlag Anton Schroll & Co., Vienna, Austria and Munich, West Germany)
p. 44	Matthias Grünewald, Angel Concert, Isenheim Altar – Musée d'Unterlinden, Société Schongauer, Colmar, France
p. 45	Matthias Grünewald, Detail from Anthony in Temptation, Isenheim Altar – Musée d'Unterlinden, Société Schongauer, Colmar, France
p. 48	Stefan Lochner, Detail from The Last Judgment – Wallraf-Richartz-Museum, Cologne, West Germany
pp. 54, 62	Hugo van der Goes, Detail from The Death of Mary – Ernst Günther Grimme, UNSERE LIEBE FRAU (DuMont Buchverlag, Cologne, West Germany, 1968)
pp. 56, 57	Tapisserie de l'Apocalypse d'Angers, The Shipwreck, Babylon Captured by the Demons, The Believers at the River of the Water of Life – Service photographiques de la Caisse Nationale des Monuments Historiques, Paris, France © C.N.M.H.S./S.P.A.D.E.M.

pp. 58, 59	Hans Memling, Christ Surrounded by Angels Who Are Singing and Making Music – Koninklijk Museum voor Schone Kunsten, Antwerp, Belgium
pp. 60, 61	Fra Angelico, Detail from The Coronation of Mary – Scala Istituto Fotografico Editoriale, Antella, Florence, Italy
p. 69	Fra Angelico, The Crucified Lord – Scala Istituto Fotografico Editoriale, Antella, Florence, Italy
p. 70	Fra Angelico, Detail from The Last Judgment – Scala Istituto Fotografico Editoriale, Antella, Florence, Italy
p. 71	Oberrheinischer Meister, Little Garden of Paradise, DIE BLAUEN BÜCHER, MARIA IM ROSENHAG (Verlag Karl Robert Langewiesche, Nachfolger Hans Köster, Königstein, West Germany, 1959)
p. 73	Meister von Moulins, Detail from The Coronation of Mary – Ernst Günther Grimme, UNSERE LIEBE FRAU (DuMont Buchverlag, Cologne, West Germany, 1968)
p. 74	Christ and the Sleeping Disciple, Sigmaringen – Bildarchiv Foto Marburg, West Germany

All other photos and illustrations – Evangelical Sisterhood of Mary, Darmstadt, West Germany

There are more books by MOTHER BASILEA SCHLINK!

You will certainly be interested in reading REALITIES, which was mentioned in one of the stories.

REALITIES – THE MIRACLES OF GOD EXPERIENCED TODAY (128 pages)

Responses: "I was thrilled to read REALITIES. It is not only exciting to read, but it also makes you want to try out prayer and faith right away..." "I never would have thought that God gives us what we ask of Him if we believe in Him with all our heart."

Your parents, relatives or teachers may like to read these books:

PATMOS – WHEN THE HEAVENS OPENED (128 pages)
The Revelation of John comes alive in the events of our times

FATHER OF COMFORT (128 pages)
A word of comfort for every day of the year

MORE PRECIOUS THAN GOLD (224 pages)
God's commandments – a present for every single day of the year

REPENTANCE – THE JOY-FILLED LIFE (62 pages)
Repentance – a golden key that opens the door to a joy-filled life

MY ALL FOR HIM (160 pages)
On the greatest treasure of the Christian life: love for Jesus

LET ME STAND AT YOUR SIDE (160 pages)
A Passion narrative that movingly takes us into the events of Maundy Thursday and Good Friday as if we were there

A FORETASTE OF HEAVEN (autobiography, 416 pages)
(American title: I FOUND THE KEY TO THE HEART OF GOD)
A tremendous source of encouragement to the Christian